WITHDRAWN

# Mexican American

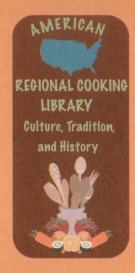

AMERICAN

REGIONAL COOKING
LIBRARY
Culture, Tradition,
and History

*Mexican American*

Mason Crest Publishers

Philadelphia

Mason Crest Publishers Inc.
370 Reed Road, Broomall, Pennsylvania 19008
(866) MCP-BOOK (toll free)
www.masoncrest.com

First Edition, 2005
13 12 11 10 09 08 07 06          10 9 8 7 6 5 4 3 2

Library of Congress Cataloging-in-Publication Data

Mexican American.
      p. cm. — (American regional cooking library)
   Includes bibliographical references and index.
   ISBN 1-59084-622-2
   1.  Cookery, American—Southwestern style—juvenile literature. 2.  Mexican American cookery—Juvenile literature.  I. Series.
   TX715.2.S69M475 2005
   641.59'26872073—dc22
                                2004016695

Dishes prepared by Juan Valazquez, Margarita's Mexican Grill, Endicott, New York
Produced by Harding House Publishing Services, Inc., Vestal, New York.
www.hardinghousepages.com
Interior design by Dianne Hodack.
Cover design by Michelle Bouch.
Printed and bound in the Hashemite Kingdom of Jordan.

# Contents

# Introduction
### by the Culinary Institute of America

Cooking is a dynamic profession, one that presents some of the greatest challenges and offers some of the greatest rewards. Since 1946, the Culinary Institute of America has provided aspiring and seasoned food service professionals with the knowledge and skills needed to become leaders and innovators in this industry.

Here at the CIA, we teach our students the fundamental culinary techniques they need to build a sound foundation for their food service careers. There is always another level of perfection for them to achieve and another skill to master. Our rigorous curriculum provides them with a springboard to continued growth and success.

Food is far more than simply sustenance or the source of energy to fuel you and your family through life's daily regimen. It conjures memories throughout life, summoning up the smell, taste, and flavor of simpler times. Cooking is more than an art and a science; it provides family history. Food prepared with care epitomizes the love, devotion, and culinary delights that you offer to your friends and family.

A cuisine provides a way to express and establish customs—the way a food should taste and the flavors and aromas associated with that food. Cuisines are more than just a collection of ingredients, cooking utensils, and dishes from a geographic location; they are elements that are critical to establishing a culinary identity.

When you can accurately read a recipe, you can trace a variety of influences by observing which ingredients are selected and also by noting the technique that is used. If you research the historical origins of a recipe, you may find ingredients that traveled from East to West or from the New World to the Old. Traditional methods of cooking a dish may have changed with the times or to meet special challenges.

The history of cooking illustrates the significance of innovation and the trading or sharing of ingredients and tools between societies. Although the various cooking vessels over the years have changed, the basic cooking methods have remained the same. Through adaptation, a recipe created years ago in a remote corner of the world could today be recognized by many throughout the globe.

When observing the customs of different societies, it becomes apparent that food brings people together. It is the common thread that we share and that we value. Regardless of the occasion, food is present to celebrate and to comfort. Through food we can experience other cultures and lands, learning the significance of particular ingredients and cooking techniques.

As you begin your journey through the culinary arts, keep in mind the power that food and cuisine holds. When passed from generation to generation, family heritage and traditions remain strong. Become familiar with the dishes your family has enjoyed through the years and play a role in keeping them alive. Don't be afraid to embellish recipes along the way – creativity is what cooking is all about.

# Mexican American Culture, History, and Traditions

The Mexican American food we know today started with the Aztecs, who were growing corn and preparing tamales and tortillas long before Spanish explorers arrived in 1519. As Mexico's original native cuisine, Aztec cooking formed the foundation for later Mexican cooking.

Without the convenience of electric appliances, cooking was very hard work, but the native Mexicans invented equipment for mashing and grilling and found ways to season food and make it taste better. Using the *metate*, a flat, slanted grinding stone, they ground chilies, tomatoes, cornmeal, or pumpkinseeds into thick sauces they called *molli*. Seasoned beans simmered slowly in clay pots set over hot coals. Mashing chilies and tart fruits called *tomatillos* with avocado flavored their guacamole. Wrapping food in leaves gave it a special flavor while roasting. Tamales were steamed in cornhusks.

When the Spanish conquered and colonized Mexico, they brought with them new ingredients, recipes, and food preparation methods. The Spanish had come to Mexico not only for wealth, but to spread the Roman Catholic religion. As friars, monks, priests, and nuns brought Christianity, European customs and cookery accompanied them. Monks and nuns arriving in New Spain to spread Christianity brought their European cooking techniques. Their kitchens mixed Spanish and native cuisines, and traditional Indian foods took new twists.

The Spanish also changed the way native Mexicans ate by importing the first domestic animals to Mexico. Eventually, the Indians acquired a taste for beef, pork, and chicken, and worked them into native recipes; for example, they began making tamales with pork fat.

In the 1840s and 1850s, when the United States gained huge pieces of what had been Mexican territory, some of the first things Americans noticed about their new neighbors were their unusual and tasty foods. By the end of the nineteenth century, Mexican foods were being incorporated into a few American cookbooks. As the years went by, many Mexican foods were adapted to appeal to American tastes—foods like

chili, tortilla chips, and nachos. Over the past fifty years, Mexican American foods were commercialized, and both sit-down and fast-food Mexican restaurants have spread across the United States.

Today, Mexican American foods add rich diversity to American cuisine. Both their convenience and their taste have made their popularity skyrocket. Try out a few of these delicious dishes. Take a taste of Mexican America!

# Before you cook...

If you haven't done much cooking before, you may find recipe books a little confusing. Certain words and terms can seem unfamiliar. You may find the measurements difficult to understand. What appears to be an easy or familiar dish may contain ingredients you've never heard of before. You might not understand what utensil the recipe calls for you to use, or you might not be sure what the recipe is asking you to do.

Reading the pages in this section before you get started may help you understand the directions better so that your cooking goes more smoothly. You can also refer back to these pages whenever you run into questions.

## Safety Tips

Cooking involves handling very hot and very sharp objects, so being careful is common sense. What's more, you want to be certain that anything you plan on putting in your mouth is safe to eat. If you follow these easy tips, you should find that cooking can be both fun and safe.

# *Before you cook...*

- Always wash your hands before and after handling food. This is particularly important after you handle raw meats, poultry, and eggs, as bacteria called salmonella can live on these uncooked foods. You can't see or smell salmonella, but these germs can make you or anyone who swallows them very sick.
- Make a habit of using potholders or oven mitts whenever you handle pots and pans from the oven or microwave.
- Always set pots, pans, and knives with their handles away from counter edges. This way you won't risk catching your sleeves on them—and any younger children in the house won't be in danger of grabbing something hot or sharp.
- Don't leave perishable food sitting out of the refrigerator for more than an hour or two.
- Wash all raw fruits and vegetables to remove dirt and chemicals.
- Use a cutting board when chopping vegetables or fruit, and always cut away from yourself.
- Don't overheat grease or oil—but if grease or oil does catch fire, don't try to extinguish the flames with water. Instead, throw baking soda or salt on the fire to put it out. Turn all stove burners off.
- If you burn yourself, immediately put the burn under cold water, as this will prevent the burn from becoming more painful.
- Never put metal dishes or utensils in the microwave. Use only microwave-proof dishes.
- Wash cutting boards and knives thoroughly after cutting meat, fish or poultry — especially when raw and before using the same tools to prepare other foods such as vegetables and cheese. This will prevent the spread of bacteria such as salmonella.
- Keep your hands away from any moving parts of appliances, such as mixers.
- Unplug any appliance, such as a mixer, blender, or food processor before assembling for use or disassembling after use.

# *Metric Conversion Table*

Most cooks in the United States use measuring containers based on an eight-ounce cup, a teaspoon, and a tablespoon. Meanwhile, cooks in Canada and Europe are more apt to use metric measurements. The recipes in this book use cups, teaspoons, and tablespoons—but you can convert these measurements to metric by using the table below.

Temperature
To convert Fahrenheit degrees to Celsius, subtract 32 and multiply by .56.

212°F = 100°C
(this is the boiling point of water)
250°F = 110°C
275°F = 135°C
300°F = 150°C
325°F = 160°C
350°F = 180°C
375°F = 190°C
400°F = 200°C

Liquid Measurements
1 teaspoon = 5 milliliters
1 tablespoon = 15 milliliters
1 fluid ounce = 30 milliliters
1 cup = 240 milliliters
1 pint = 480 milliliters
1 quart = 0.95 liters
1 gallon = 3.8 liters

Measurements of Mass or Weight
1 ounce = 28 grams
8 ounces = 227 grams
1 pound (16 ounces) = 0.45 kilograms
2.2 pounds = 1 kilogram

Measurements of Length
¼ inch = 0.6 centimeters
½ inch = 1.25 centimeters
1 inch = 2.5 centimeters

# Pan Sizes

Baking pans are usually made in standard sizes. The pans used in the United States are roughly equivalent to the following metric pans:

9-inch cake pan = 23-centimeter pan
11x7-inch baking pan = 28x18-centimeter baking pan
13x9-inch baking pan = 32.5x23-centimeter baking pan
9x5-inch loaf pan = 23x13-centimeter loaf pan
2-quart casserole = 2-liter casserole

# Useful Tools, Utensils, Dishes

basting brush

blender

casserole

cheese grater

pastry cutter

potato masher

rolling pin      saucepan      skillet

slotted spoon      spatula

# *Cooking Glossary*

*broil*  To cook in the oven by direct exposure to heat.

*cut*  To mix dry ingredients with semisolid ones with a fork or pastry cutter.

*diced*  Cut into small cubes or pieces.

*marinade*  A savory sauce in which meat is soaked to flavor and tenderize it.

*marinate*  To soak in a marinade.

*minced*  Cut into very small pieces.

*pinch*  An amount that equals less than 1/4 teaspoon.

*sauté*  Fry in a skillet or frying pan with a little oil or butter.

*simmer*  Gently boil, so that the surface of the liquid just ripples gently.

*stock*  A liquid in which meat, fish, or vegetables have been simmered, used as a base for gravy, soup, or sauce.

*toss*  Turn food over quickly and lightly so that it is evenly covered with a liquid or powder.

*whisk*  To mix or fluff up by beating briskly.

# *Special Mexican American Flavors*

bell pepper

cayenne

chilies

cilantro

cumin

garlic

green onions

tomatillos

# Mexican American Recipes

# Flour Tortillas

*Tortillas are the main ingredients of Mexican American food. Of course, you can buy them ready-made—but for a genuine Mexican experience, try making your own.*

## Ingredients:

2 cups flour
1 teaspoon salt
⅓ cup vegetable shortening
½ cup warm water

*Cooking utensils you'll need:*
*measuring cups*
*measuring spoons*
*mixing bowl*
*rolling pin*
*skillet or frying pan*
*spatula*

## Directions:

Mix together flour and salt in a bowl. **Cut** in the shortening, and then add water to make a stiff dough. Knead on a lightly floured board. Form dough into 8 small balls and let dough stand 15 minutes. With a heavy wooden rolling pin, roll balls to paper-thin thickness and brown in a lightly greased skillet. Turn with spatula. Eat—or cool and store for later use in a sealed plastic bag.

## Mexican American Food History

Before the arrival of Europeans, Mexicans ate tortillas—thin corn pancakes—alone or used them as the basis for more complex dishes. The Spanish, however, preferred breads baked with wheat flour, the kind they had eaten at home. Because the Catholic Church considered wheat the only acceptable grain for Communion wafers, the Spanish missionaries to Mexico wanted to replace native grains with wheat flour. The Europeans also believed wheat was more nutritious than corn. The natives loved corn, however, and at first the Spanish couldn't even give away wheat bread to beggars. Colonists planted wheat fields, though, and eventually, the Indians who tended them ate the bread they received as wages. Today, flour tortillas remain popular throughout modern Mexico, especially in the north, but corn tortillas are still preferred throughout much of Mexico. Americans like both, and today the tortilla has gained new popularity along with a new name—the "wrap."

## Mexican American Food Culture

Tortilla chips aren't as common across the border in Mexico—but in the United States, they've become nearly as popular as potato chips. People eat them as snacks, with meals, and in restaurants; they eat them with Mexican American food and with hamburgers and hot dogs.

American Cinco de Mayo (seen-coh day my-oh; "Fifth of May") celebrations are one occasion where you're sure to find plenty of tortilla chips (as well as lots of other food). Many Americans think that the Cinco de Mayo is Mexico's independence day, the Latino version of the Fourth July. Actually, however, the date marks the anniversary of a battle against the French during a brief period in the 1860s when France ruled Mexico. Four thousand Mexicans were victorious against twice as many French soldiers, an example of bravery and determination against seemingly impossible odds. That's why Cinco de Mayo is more than a good reason to party; it's a time to reflect on the true meaning of courage and freedom.

# Homemade Tortilla Chips

*Any grocery store has shelves full of ready-made tortilla chips—but homemade are even better.*

## Ingredients:

12 corn tortillas, cut into quarters
vegetable oil
1 teaspoon salt

**Cooking utensils you'll need:**
*measuring spoon*
*heavy pot*
*slotted spoon*

## Directions:

Add enough oil to come halfway up the sides of a large heavy pot heat over high heat. (If you use a cooking thermometer, it should be 360 degrees; otherwise, oil is hot when a drop of water sizzles when it's dropped on the surface.) In batches, without crowding, deep-fry the tortillas until golden brown, turning once, for 2 to 3 minutes. Using a slotted spoon, transfer to paper towels to drain. Sprinkle lightly with salt while still hot, and serve immediately.

# Rice and Beans

*After the tortilla, rice and beans are the most common Mexican American foods. They're found as side dishes for nearly every main course.*

## Ingredients:

*1 cup rice*
*1 onion, chopped*
*4 tablespoons olive oil*
*three fifteen-ounce cans of pinto beans*
*1½ cups of cooked rice*
*1 can of diced tomatoes*
*1 teaspoon cayenne pepper*
*1 teaspoon chili powder*

*2 cloves of garlic, minced*
*1 green pepper, diced*
*1 red pepper, diced*
*½ jalapeno pepper, minced (optional)*
*½ teaspoon cumin*
*½ teaspoon pepper*
*1 teaspoon salt*

## Directions:

Prepare the rice in a saucepan according to package directions. If you want to give it a genuine Mexican American flavor, when the rice is almost done, stir in a tablespoon of salsa or a teaspoon of chopped fresh cilantro. Meanwhile, *sauté* the onions in a large skillet until they're translucent. Add the remaining ingredients. Cover and cook on low heat for at least 40 to 45 minutes. (The longer you let the beans cook, the mushier they'll be. You can mash them with a potato masher to give them the soupy consistency of "refried beans." Serve side-by-side with the rice.

## Mexican American Food History

The history of Mexican food is intertwined with Mexico's political history. Before the Europeans' arrival, the two main food staples of native Mexicans were maize (corn) and beans. These foods have complementary amino acids that make for a nutritious combination; eating them kept Mexicans healthy for centuries, and they sometimes referred to these foods as their "mothers."

When the first Spanish Conquistadors arrived in 1519, they brought with them a new supply of protein sources: cattle, pigs, sheep, goats, and chickens, as well as new condiments: olive oil, cinnamon, parsley, coriander, oregano, and black pepper. They also introduced rice. Gradually, Mexicans combined their old ways of eating with the new ways, and rice became as common fare as corn had been. Unfortunately, however, white rice is not as nutritious as corn, and it does not combine with beans to make the same healthy amino acids. As a result, the health of native Mexicans sometimes suffered, especially when they were too poor to eat meat often.

# Tacos

## Ingredients:

2 tablespoons cooking oil
2 pounds ground beef
1 teaspoon salt
2 tablespoons chili powder (less if you don't like "hot" foods)
1 teaspoon cumin
1 teaspoon garlic powder or 2 **diced** garlic cloves
½ medium onion, chopped
¼ cup chopped fresh cilantro
½ medium bell pepper, chopped
2 cups shredded cheese (cheddar or Monterey Jack
       works well)
1 cup shredded lettuce
1 cup tomatoes, cut in small pieces
8 corn or flour tortillas

*Cooking utensils you'll need:*
*measuring cups*
*measuring spoons*
*cheese grater*
*sharp knife for cutting lettuce and tomatoes*
*frying pan or skillet*

## Directions:

Heat oil in skillet over medium high heat; then add meat and spices. When meat is brown, add onion, cilantro, and pepper, and continue cooking 20 or 30 more minutes. Drain off grease. Place a spoonful of meat in the middle of a tortilla and add cheese, tomato, and lettuce. Fold over tortilla and serve.

## Tip:

To remove fat from meat, place your skillet in the freezer for a few minutes. When grease separates and starts to harden, take a spoon and remove.

## Mexican American Food History

In Mexico, tacos are sold by vendors or in small restaurants called *taquerías*. Vendors may do business on the streets, near the entrance of a public building, or outside the church on a feast day. Today, in the United States, tacos have become common fare at fast-food restaurants, family dinners, and school cafeterias. You may be most familiar with the kind of taco that comes in a hard corn tortilla—but a true Mexican taco is seldom crunchy.

The world's largest taco was made from a tortilla that measured 14½ feet across. The townspeople of Oaxaca, Mexico, constructed it as a challenge in May 2000. Later, they filled it with 70 pounds of cheese and beef, 54 pounds of beans, and 5 gallons of salsa. That's a big taco!

# Chicken Quesadillas

## Ingredients:

2 tablespoons vegetable oil
1 pound boneless, skinless chicken breast halves, cut into thin strips
1 teaspoon salt
1 teaspoon chili powder (less if you don't like "hot" foods)
½ teaspoon cumin
1 teaspoon garlic powder
⅓ cup water
10 six-inch flour tortillas
2½ cups shredded cheddar cheese

*Cooking utensils you'll need:*
*measuring spoons*
*sharp knife for cutting chicken*
*measuring cups*
*frying pan or skillet*

## Directions:

Heat 1 tablespoon of the vegetable oil in large skillet over medium-high heat. Add chicken and cook, stirring occasionally, for 4 to 5 minutes or until chicken is no longer pink. Stir in seasoning mix and water. Bring to a boil. Reduce heat to low; cook for 3 to 4 minutes more. Then put ½ cup meat pieces on one tortilla and sprinkle with ½ cup cheese. Place second tortilla evenly over mixture. Heat remaining oil in large skillet over medium-high heat. Place quesadilla in skillet; cook for 2 to 3 minutes on each side or until golden brown and cheese is melted. Repeat with remaining ingredients. Makes 4 servings.

## Tip:

You can buy ready-made spice packets for seasoning Mexican foods.

## Mexican American Food History

A Mexican saying, "*se me antojó*," describes a sudden, fanciful craving for a snack. The best known of all Mexican foods, *antojitos* are literally "little whims." Usually antojitos mean corn-based items, the tacos, quesadillas, and enchiladas so familiar to Americans.

# Enchilados and Salsa Verde

*Enchilados are made by wrapping cheese and/or precooked chicken in corn tortillas. They are placed in a baking dish and covered with either* salsa roja *(a red tomato-based sauce) or* salsa verde *(green sauce), and baked. Here is the recipe for salsa verde.*

**Preheat oven to 350 degrees Fahrenheit.**

## Ingredients:

½ large green pepper, chopped
1 long chili
1 or more small hot green chilies
5 to 6 tomatillos
1 stalk of celery, chopped fine
¼ cup chopped fresh cilantro
1 large onion, **diced**
1 to 2 green onions, chopped fine
2 tablespoons olive oil
½ teaspoon cumin
4 to 5 cloves of garlic, diced
2 tablespoons sugar
juice from 3 limes (about ¼ cup)
2 cups chicken **stock** or broth
salt and pepper to taste

*Cooking utensils you'll need:*
*measuring spoons*
*measuring cups*
*sharp knife*
*heavy skillet*

## Directions:

Chop the peppers, chilies, tomatillos (remove the husks), celery, cilantro, and onions. Heat the oil in a large frying pan or skillet, and then *sauté* the chilies, tomatillos, onion, garlic, celery, and green pepper until they are soft. Add the cumin and cilantro and sauté for another 2 or 3 minutes. Add the remaining ingredients, stir, and bring to a gentle boil. Reduce heat and *simmer*, stirring now and then to keep it from sticking. When the sauce is thick, remove from heat. If you want a smooth texture, process it in a blender. Pour over enchilados and bake for about half an hour, until the enchilados are beginning to brown. Serve hot with rice, beans, and sour cream.

## Tips:

You can omit the chilies (or use smaller portions) if you don't like spicy foods. If you do use chili peppers, be careful not to touch your eyes while handling them and wash your skin thoroughly wherever it comes in contact with the chilies.

Canned chicken broth is a good substitute for chicken stock.

### Mexican American Food History

Tomatillos look like tiny green tomatoes, but they are actually in the gooseberry family. Native to Mexico, they have been adding tang to Mexican dishes for centuries.

# Fajitas

## Ingredients:

1 pound chicken breast cut in strips
½ cup cooking oil
1 tablespoon chili powder
1 clove garlic, **minced**
2 tablespoons cumin
1 onion cut in strips
1 green pepper cut in strips
1 pound Monterey Jack cheese, grated
2 cups shredded lettuce
6 green onions chopped
8 flour tortillas

*Cooking utensils you'll need:*
*measuring cups*
*measuring spoons*
*sharp knife for cutting meat and vegetables*
*cheese grater*
*large skillet or frying pan*

## Directions:

*Marinate* chicken in the oil, chili powder, garlic, and cumin for several hours. For best results, refrigerate overnight. Place the chicken, onion, and pepper in skillet and cook until chicken is no longer pink and vegetables are soft. Warm tortillas in the stove or microwave. Place several slices of meat, cheese, onions and peppers, and lettuce in each tortilla, and wrap tortilla around the mixture. Serve with sour cream and salsa (see page 39).

## Tips:

You can also make steak fajitas, preparing the beef the same way you did the chicken.

To heat tortillas, wrap the stack in a clean dishtowel and place on an oven-proof/microwave-proof plate. Heat for 1 or 2 minutes at high in the microwave or for 10 minutes in a 300-degree oven.

### Mexican American Food History

The original fajitas (fah-hee-tahs) were made from steak in South Texas in the 1930s. The word comes from *faja*, the Spanish term for a particular cut of beef. Ranch workers would tenderize the meat by pounding it and then marinating it in lime juice. The meat would be sliced and cooked over an open fire.

# Salsa

*You can buy ready-made salsa in your grocery store—but homemade salsa is tastier and richer in vitamins and fiber.*

## Ingredients:

*3 or 4 medium-size tomatoes*
*3 or 4 tomatillos with the husks removed (if you don't have tomatillos, you can use*
*2 more tomatoes)*
*6 to 8 garlic cloves*
*4 to 6 serrano chilies (optional)*
*1 medium white onion, chopped*
*1 small bunch of cilantro*
*2 teaspoons salt*
*juice from one lime*

*Cooking utensils you'll need:*
*measuring spoons*
*blender*

## Directions:

Place ingredients a little at a time in the blender and blend until coarsely chopped. Let the salsa stand for at least an hour at room temperature to allow the flavors to combine. Leftovers will keep for several days if covered tightly and refrigerated.

## Mexican American Food Fact

Here's a good indication of Mexican food's popularity: Americans today buy more salsa than they do ketchup.

# Easy Guacamole

## Ingredients:

2 large avocados
2 teaspoons lemon juice
⅓ cup salsa

**Cooking utensils you'll need:**
measuring spoons
measuring cups
sharp knife
fork

## Directions:

Cut avocados in half and scoop out the green flesh. In a medium bowl, mash avocados with a fork. Add lemon juice and salsa; stir until blended.

## Mexican American Food History

Guacamole is an ancient Mexican food. Avocado seeds have been found in archeological sites dating back to 6,000 B.C.E.— and according to historical records, the Aztecs made a sauce from avocados that they called *ahuaca-mulli* . . . guacamole, in other words. Just like today, it consisted of mashed avocados mixed with chopped tomatoes and onions.

# Carne Asada

## Ingredients:

1½ pounds top round steak or boneless chuck steak, cut 1½ inches thick
¼ cup red wine vinegar
2 tablespoons olive oil
1 teaspoon cilantro
1 teaspoon cumin
½ teaspoon salt
¼ teaspoon cayenne pepper (optional)
½ teaspoon paprika

*Cooking utensils you'll need:*
*measuring cups*
*measuring spoons*
*basting brush*

## Directions:

Allow meat to *marinate* in other ingredients for at least 6 hours (or overnight in the refrigerator). Barbecue meat or broil in the oven, brushing occasionally with the *marinade*. Cook 30 to 40 minutes, turning once. Serve with onions, salsa, and tortillas.

## Mexican American Food Fact

*Carne asada* (car-nay ah-sah-dah) means simply "roasted meat."

# Chicken Burrito

## Ingredients:

1 chicken breast
1 teaspoon salsa
½ teaspoon cumin
1 large flour tortilla
1 wheat tortilla

## Directions:

Broil the chicken breast until the meat is no longer pink. (Don't allow meat to brown or dry out.) *Shred* the chicken breast and add a little salsa and cumin for flavor. The amount depends on your taste. Warm the flour tortilla in the microwave or oven (see page 37). Put the shredded chicken breast on one end of the tortilla, fold the sides over, and roll into a cylinder. Serve with refried beans and Mexican rice. Makes a single serving, so multiply ingredients by however many people you want to feed.

### Mexican American Food History

*Burrito* (boo-ree-toh) means literally "little burro" or "little donkey." The burrito originated in the southwestern borderlands between Tucson and Los Angeles. This hearty and simple ranch-style food showcases the region's flavorful beef. The word first appeared in print in the United States in 1934, and it entered mainstream Mexican American cuisine in the 1960s.

## Mexican American Food History

Chilies are a true food of the Americas. Many thousands of years ago, the plant that ultimately produced all members of the pepper family, both hot and sweet, originated in what is today Bolivia. From there it made its way to Mexico. Long-ago Mexicans portrayed the chili pepper in pottery and tapestries. It even functioned as a form of currency. Today, there are many varieties of peppers, ranging from hot to mild.

Some of the most common varieties of Mexican peppers:

| | | | |
|---|---|---|---|
| bell | Fresno | pimentos | poblanos |
| ancho | Serrano | yellow | habanero |

# Chili Relleno

Chili relleno *(chee-lee ray-yay-no) means "stuffed chili."*

## Ingredients:

6 green peppers
½ teaspoon salt
1 cup shredded Monterey Jack cheese
1 cup flour
2 large eggs
3 tablespoons cooking oil
1 can tomato sauce
½ pound ground beef
3 tablespoons chopped onion
1 **minced** garlic clove
3-ounce can of tomatoes and green chili peppers
¼ cup water if needed

*Cooking utensils you'll need:*
*measuring cups*
*measuring spoons*
*cheese grater*
*sharp knife*
*large frying pan*

## Directions:

**Broil** peppers until skin is bubbly. Remove peppers from oven and put in plastic bag. Let cool and then peel outer layer of skin. Slice down one side and remove seeds. Stuff with cheese. Coat generously with flour. Beat eggs and dip stuffed peppers into egg mixture. Fry in hot oil until golden brown on both sides. Brown meat and onions. Add remaining ingredients and *simmer* for 15 minutes.

# *Calabacitas*

## *Ingredients:*

*1 tablespoon olive oil*
*1 large onion, chopped*
*3 cloves garlic, minced*
*4 small zucchini or summer squash, sliced*
*½ teaspoon salt, or to taste*

***Cooking utensils you'll need:***
*measuring spoons*
*sharp knife for cutting onion, garlic, and squash*
*measuring spoons*
*large skillet or frying pan*

## *Directions:*

Heat olive oil in a large skillet over medium-high heat. Add onion and garlic, and cook, stirring until translucent. Add zucchini and *sauté* until soft. Season with salt. Serve with rice and beans.

## *Mexican American Food History*

*Calabacitas* (cah-lah-bah-see-tahs)—"little squash"—are another ancient Mexican food. But how do we know what the long-ago Mexicans ate?

We know about the Aztecs' food from descriptions written by Cortés and his companions, who were astonished by all they saw. We also know about the Aztecs' cuisine because it continues to be practiced. Through the centuries, residents of small villages have continued making tortillas and tamales in the old way. Chefs and cookbook authors have visited Mexican communities to research recipes passed down through generations. In addition, modern researchers can identify ingredients used in ancient foods by studying residue on pottery fragments.

# Ensalada de Nopalitos (Cactus Salad)

*Nopalitos are available in cans and jars, as well as fresh.*

## Ingredients:

3 cups nopalitos, chopped
3 tablespoons onion, chopped
½ cup cilantro, chopped
2 tablespoons fresh lime juice
½ cup sliced black olives
2 cups tomatoes, chopped

**Cooking utensils you'll need:**
*measuring cups*
*measuring spoons*
*large mixing bowl*

## Directions:

Mix ingredients in a large mixing bowl and allow to sit for 30 minutes.

## Tip:

Serve topped with diced tomatoes, shredded cheese, jalapeño peppers, and/or avocado slices.

## Mexican American Food History

*Nopalitos* (no-pah-lee-toes) is another word for prickly pear cactus. (You don't eat the prickers, of course.) This cactus is yet another food native to Mexico; the plants were being grown and eaten before the Spanish arrived. The Spanish brought the plant with them back to Europe, where it spread from Spain to North Africa.

# Nachos

## Ingredients:

1 pound ground beef
1 teaspoon cumin
½ teaspoon cayenne pepper
**pinch** of salt and pepper
36 tortilla chips
2½ cups refried beans
4 cups shredded Cheddar cheese
1 onion, finely chopped
2 tomatoes, **diced**
1 jalapeño chili, sliced (optional)
1 small container of sour cream

*Cooking utensils you'll need:*
*measuring cups*
*sharp knife for cutting onion, tomatoes, and chilies*
*frying pan*
*cheese grater*
*large ovenproof plates*

## Directions:

Place the ground beef and seasonings in a frying pan over medium high heat and cook until it is brown. Drain off any fat. Spread the tortilla chips on 2 microwavable or ovenproof platters or large plates. Spread the beans on top of the chips and top with the ground beef. Sprinkle with the cheese.

Place 1 microwavable plate in the microwave and heat for 30 seconds, or until the cheese has melted. Or place the ovenproof plate in the preheated oven and heat for 3 to 5 minutes. Top with half of the onion, tomatoes, and chili. Place dollops of sour cream on top, and serve immediately. Repeat with the second plate of nachos.

## Mexican American Food History

Tortilla chips were originally made from leftover tortillas that had been cut up and baked or fried. These chips soon became a staple in Mexican American restaurants, but they never really caught on in Mexico.

Nachos are another food invention that became popular first in the United States rather than Mexico. According to one story, a man named Ignacio Ahaya, whose nickname was Nacho, was asked to prepare a snack for some officers' wives on a military base. He grabbed a bunch of tortillas, put some cheese on top, heated it, and sliced jalapeños on top. Nachos quickly spread throughout Texas, and by the 1980s, they had become a popular snack throughout the United States. Today, they've become traditional fare at Super Bowl parties.

# Chimichangas

*Preheat oven to 375 degrees Fahrenheit*

## Ingredients:

*3-pound boneless shoulder chuck roast*
*salt and pepper to taste*
*2 tablespoons vegetable oil*
*3 garlic cloves, **minced***
*½ cup chopped onion*
*1 cup beef **stock***
*10 tortillas*
*cooking oil*

*Cooking utensils you'll need:*
*frying pan or skillet*
*measuring spoons*
*sharp knife for cutting onion and garlic*
*measuring cups*
*Dutch oven or large pan*

## Directions:

Rub the salt and pepper on the roast. Sauté in the oil and add onion, garlic, and beef broth. Cover tightly and simmer for about 1½ hours, until roast is very tender. Cool until you can handle the roast. Use two forks to shred the beef into small pieces. Add the meat to the broth and add another ½ cup diced onion. Cook until all liquid is out of the beef. The beef should remain moist but not juicy. Warm the tortillas enough so that you can roll them. Place ¾ cup of the meat mixture in the center of the tortilla. Fold in sides and roll up. Secure with toothpicks.

Heat 5 inches of oil in Dutch oven or other large pan. Place the rolled up tortillas in the oil and fry until golden brown, about 4 minutes. Drain on paper towels and top with cheese, sour cream, salsa, and green onions. Serve immediately.

## Tips:

You can use canned beef broth in place of beef stock.

You can tell when oil is hot enough to fry because it will sizzle if you drop a bead of water into it. Be very careful when working with hot oil; it tends to spit, which can burn your skin and stain your clothes. Always be sure that any pan handles are turned away from the edge of the stove, so that younger children do not grab them and burn themselves.

## Mexican American Food History

*Chimichanga* (chee-mee-chahn-gah) is a Mexican nonsense word, sort of a Spanish version of "whatchamacallit," "do-hickey" or "thingamajig." According to culinary historians, the term was first used for a Tex-Mex food in the 1950s in Tucson, Arizona. The story goes that the first chimichanga was created when a burrito was accidentally knocked into a deep-fat fryer. The cook exclaimed "Chimichanga!"—and both the word and the food became popular fare.

# Mexican Chicken

*Preheat oven to 375 degrees Fahrenheit*

## Ingredients:

*1 cup rice*
*1⅔ cups chicken broth*
*½ cup chopped onion*
*½ teaspoon salt, or to taste*
*4 chicken pieces*
*1 cup chunky salsa*
*package of frozen peas (optional)*

*Cooking utensils you'll need:*
*measuring cups*
*measuring spoons*
*sharp knife for chopping onion*
*casserole*

## Directions:

In a large pan, bring chicken broth to a boil. Add rice, onions, peas, and salt; boil 10 minutes and then remove from the heat. Place rice in a lightly buttered casserole dish with chicken pieces on top and pour salsa over everything. Cover tightly and bake at 350° until the chicken's juices run clear when you stick it with a fork or knife (about 55 minutes to an hour).

## Mexican American Food Tradition

To be a good woman in nineteenth-century Mexico meant you had a profound knowledge of food. Mexican women ran their homes and cooked their families' meals with both skill and imagination. Their gift for improvisation—creating new dishes out of whatever ingredients they had on hand—contributed much to today's Mexican American food. The modern world-wide demand for their delicious dishes is a testament to their talent.

# Chili con Queso

Chili con queso *(chee-lee cone kay-so) means chili with cheese. Among Mexican Americans, it's a popular dip for tortillas.*

## Ingredients:

4-ounce can of chopped green chilies, drained
2 tablespoons onion, finely chopped
2 teaspoons cumin
½ teaspoon salt
1 cup shredded cheese (either cheddar or Monterey Jack)

*Cooking utensils you'll need:*
*measuring cups*
*measuring spoons*
*microwave or ovenproof dish*

## Directions:

Mix chilies and seasonings together and place in microwave-safe dish. Top with cheese.

Microwave ingredients for 3 minutes (or place in a 350-degree oven for 10 minutes), or until cheese is melted. Serve warm with tortilla chips.

## Mexican American Food Culture

Some of the most popular Mexican American foods are Tex-Mex dishes. This cuisine is rooted in a cultural blend of Northern Mexico and the American Southwest (especially southern Texas). There, Native Americans, Mexicans, Texans, and cowboys of all cultures intermingled to give us a unique food sensation.

# Taco Salad

## Ingredients:

1½ pounds ground beef
¼ cup chopped onion
½ teaspoon salt
½ teaspoon cumin
¼ teaspoon pepper
½ cup canned refried beans
½ head lettuce, shredded
2 tomatoes, cut in wedges
tortilla chips or already shaped hard tortilla
4 ounces cheddar cheese, shredded
1 cup salsa
1 cup sour cream

*Cooking utensils you'll need:*
*measuring cups*
*measuring spoons*
*knife for cutting onion and lettuce*
*cheese grater*
*frying pan or skillet*
*microwave-proof bowl or small saucepan*
*for beans*

## Directions:

Fry ground beef, onion, and seasonings in a frying pan over medium high heat until meat is brown. Drain off fat. Heat refried beans in the microwave or on the stovetop. For each serving, put lettuce on the tortilla and top with beans, meat mixture, tomato wedges, a spoonful of cheese, a spoonful of salsa, and a spoonful of sour cream.

## Mexican American Food Culture

Taco salads are an American adaptation of the classic Mexican taco. Mexican American recipes in general are a constantly evolving meld of techniques, ingredients, and flavors. As this food culture comes in contact with America's many other ethnic groups, it is changed and adapted, creating a cuisine that is dynamic and exciting.

# Mexican Hot Chocolate

## Ingredients:

½ pound semisweet chocolate chips
4 cups milk
¼ teaspoon ground cinnamon
2 drops vanilla

## Directions:

Break the chocolate into small pieces. Fill the bottom of the double boiler with cold water. Then bring the water to a boil over high heat on the stove. Turn the heat down so that the water continues to boil gently, and put the chocolate chips in the top of the double boiler, over the part with the boiling water. With a wooden spoon, stir the chocolate until it has melted. Measure out the milk and pour it into another saucepan. Heat the milk gently but do not let it boil. Pour the melted chocolate into the hot milk, along with the cinnamon and the vanilla. Bring the mixture to a boil. Then turn the heat down and *whisk* the mixture for 2 minutes until it is foaming. Pour the chocolate into mugs and use a small whisk to whisk the chocolate again, so that there is foam on the top of each mug. Makes 4 mugs.

## Mexican American Food History and Tradition

Archeologists tell us that the Mexican Olmecs, the oldest civilization of the Americas (1500–400 B.C.E.), were probably the first ones to use cocoa. Later, the Maya favored a drink called *chocolatl* that was made from roasted cocoa beans, water, and a little spice; cocoa beans were so valuable, the Maya used them instead of money.

When the Spanish conquistadors arrived in Mexico, Montezuma, Emperor of Mexico, was the one who introduced Cortes to his favorite drink served in a golden goblet. Historical records refer to Montezuma's "potation of chocolate, flavored with vanilla and spices, and so prepared as to be reduced to a froth of the consistency of honey, which gradually dissolved in the mouth and was taken cold." Cortes wrote a letter to Charles V of Spain, calling chocolate "the divine drink which builds up resistance and fights fatigue. A cup of this precious drink permits a man to walk for a whole day without food." When Cortes returned to Spain in 1528, he loaded his galleons with cocoa beans and chocolate drink-making equipment. Europeans added sugar to the concoction, and the drink became the rage across Europe.

True Mexican hot chocolate, however, is still a little different from what you're probably used to, mostly because it has cinnamon in it. Today, in central and southern Mexico, many people still drink chocolate twice a day year-round. And having a layer of foam on hot chocolate is as important today in Mexico as it was in ancient times. Mexicans believe the spirit of the drink is in the foam.

# Further Reading

Bayless, Rick. *Rick Bayless's Mexican Kitchen: Capturing the Vibrant Flavors of a World-Class Cuisine.* New York: Scribner, 1996.

Ford, Jean. *The Taste of Celebration: Latino Cuisine and Its Influence on American Foods.* Philadelphia, Penn.: Mason Crest Publishers, 2005.

Kennedy, Diana. *The Essential Cuisines of Mexico.* New York: Clarkston Potter, 2000.

Martinez, Zarela. *Food from My Heart: Cuisines of Mexico Remembered and Reimagined.* New York: Macmillan, 1992.

Pilcher, Jeffrey M. *¡Que vivan los tamales! Food and the Making of Mexican Identity.* Albuquerque: University of New Mexico Press, 1998.

Sanna, Ellyn. *Food Folklore.* Philadelphia, Penn.: Mason Crest Publishers, 2003.

# For More Information

Lo Mexicano
www.lomexicano.com/

Mexican Cuisine
www.mexico.udg.mx/cocina/ingles/ingles.html

Mexican Food and Culture
food.oregonstate.edu/ref/culture/mexico_smith.html

Mexican Food History
www.texmextogo.com/TexMexFoodHistory.htm

Mexican Recipes
mexicanfood.about.com/gi/dynamic

Publisher's note:
The Web sites listed on this page were active at the time of publication. The publisher is not responsible for Web sites that have changed their addresses or discontinued operation since the date of publication. The publisher will review and update the Web sites upon each reprint.

# Index

# *Index*

## Author:

Ellyn Sanna is the author of *101 Easy Supper Recipes for Busy Moms* from Promise Press, and several recipe gift books from Barbour Publishing, including *Feast, An Invitation to Tea*, and the books in the "Christmas at Home" series. A former middle school teacher and the mother of three children ages eleven through sixteen, she has experience addressing both the learning needs and the food tastes of young cooks. Ellyn Sanna has also authored and edited numerous educational titles.

## Food Preparer:

Margarita's Mexican Grill, a restaurant on Watson Boulevard in Endicott, New York, serves genuine Mexican food. Family owned and operated, the colorful and delicious meals demonstrate the skill of three generations of Mexican cooking, as well as forty years of experience in the food service industry. Traditional Mexican cooking uses all fresh ingredients—and so does Margarita's. Simplicity, friendliness, and flavorful cooking embody the true Mexican food experience—and Margarita's brings these qualities to life.

## Consultant:

The Culinary Institute of America is considered the world's premier culinary college. It is a private, not-for-profit learning institution, dedicated to providing the world's best culinary education. Its campuses in New York and California provide learning environments that focus on excellence, leadership, professionalism, ethics, and respect for diversity. The institute embodies a passion for food with first-class cooking expertise.

# Picture Credits